The House by the Sea.

Alpha Nu Society.
4 – 75

THE

HOUSE BY THE SEA.

A Poem.

BY

THOMAS BUCHANAN READ.

"Magic casements opening on the foam
Of perilous seas."—KEATS.

PHILADELPHIA:
PARRY & McMILLAN,
SUCCESSORS TO A. HART, LATE CAREY & HART.
1855.

STEREOTYPED BY L. JOHNSON AND CO.
PHILADELPHIA.

PRINTED BY T. K. & P. G. COLLINS.

He told a tale as wild as sad;
And they who listened deemed it mad—
Mad as the delirious dream
Of one who, on an Indian stream
Floating in a Morphean bark,
Feeds on the charméd lotus leaf—
While under the palms, in visions brief,
Through shadows of sunset, golden-dark,
The camels and camelopards stand
With pluméd tribes on the yellow sand,
To gaze with steadfast, wondering eyes
Where the feeding dreamer floating lies.

TO

Hiram Powers,

AS AN EVIDENCE OF FRIENDSHIP AND ADMIRATION,

This Poem

IS INSCRIBED BY THE AUTHOR.

Bagni di Lucca,
Sept. 1st, 1855.

THE

House by the Sea.

IN TWO PARTS.

Part First.

I.

On a little, seaward-sloping lawn,
The first bright half-hour after dawn —
With golden hair and cheeks as red
As the hue in the brightening orient spread,
The child and the light of the fisherman's home,
Bearing a pail that dript its foam
Like snowflakes on the wayside grass,
Went singing as if her soul would pass
Into the air, and o'ertake that bird
Which sang in the sky less seen than heard.

Her path was along the sweëtbrier lane,
Dividing the sea from the clover plain:

Below the billows inland bore,
And threw their foam-wreaths on the shore:
Above, the orchards, lightly blown,
Scattered their snowy garlands down,
As if the very trees would spread
A pure white path for her virgin tread.

She plucked a violet from the hedge,
And then a flower from the perilous edge
Of a cliff where foamed the sea's white ire,—
And now a bloom from the wayside brier;
Then placed them in her russet vest,
To sway to the heaving of her breast.

Descending the steep of the seaside rocks,
In pathways worn by the shepherd's flocks,
She saw the Stranger, whose cliff-perched home
Stood higher than ever the wild sea-foam
Could leap; and only the gust of spray,
Seeking the cloud, passed up that way.

It might be a moon of dawns, perchance,
Since first the stranger met her glance,
And never at any later time
Than the crimson flush of the morning's prime.
With the latest star he walked the shore,
And when that failed was seen no more.

They grew acquainted—yet did not speak:
There was a sadness on his cheek
His smile made sadder; and his look
Seemed to reflect some parchment book
Writ in a cave by a wizard gray
To spirit both body and soul away.
Her heart's deep instinct read in his eye
How he had sought that height to die;
And, as one bears flowers of sweetest bloom
To brighten a sick man's twilight room,
When now they met, with resistless grace
She stood before him—scarce looked in his face,
Tendered the blossoms, then quickened her pace.

He pressed them to his lips, and then
Strolled round to his cloudy home again.

He climbed to his gusty balcony,
That overbrowed the eastern sea:
Like a spirit in a dusky cloud,
O'erleaning the world in wonder bowed,
Pale Roland leaned, and gazed below
Into the gulfs — until on the flow
Of the billows his fancies seemed to go:
And thus to the air and the spirits of air,
Those delicate listeners everywhere,
He winged his thoughts with careless words,
Till they sailed the ocean like sea-born birds.

II.

"My house is built on the cliff's tall crest,
As high as an eagle might choose her nest:
The builders have descended the hill,
Like spirits who have done their master's will.
Below, the billows in endless reach
Commune in uncomprehended speech—
A language still—there is no sound
But symbols something though unfound.

"Here from the world I can safely lean
And feel, if not hear, what the billows mean;
And dropping this flower, I can watch it sway
Till it diminishes into the spray.
The little alien from its hillside home
Is clasped and whirled in the heartless foam!

Oh, reckless hand! it was the flower
The peasant-girl gave me this very hour!
Well, it is gone—so let it be:
Not Indus could restore to me,
With all its dew and odour fine,
Fresh and free from the bitter brine,
That victim of a heedless hand!
But it must be fretted along the sand
Till drowned and crushed, a noisome thing
At last, where the foulest seaweeds cling!

"Thus with the maid it may be, perchance,
Borne away from her vernal haunts
To make some heartless breast look bright,
Then carried to some dizzy height
And dropt from a hand relentlessly
Into the gulfs of a pitiless sea—
Into the tumultuous fret and foam
To perish—an alien far from home!

"Here I stand, like a Persian priest,
Gazing forever into the east,
And bow my head before the sun,
The symbol of a mightier One.

"Beheld from here, with march unending,
By night and by day the sky is ascending;
This is the vision of youth — the scope
Where rises the golden scale of Hope,—
When the heart in its freshness stout and hale
Recks not of the opposing scale,
Which, though unseen in the future air,
Sinks and sinks with its weight of despair.

"Nothing sets save yonder sail
Chased away by an outward gale,
And every hour to my straining gaze
Some new bark issues through the haze,—
Fresh perchance from the Orient,
Its sails with spicy breezes bent,

Like that barge on the Cydnus seen
Laden with odours that veiled a queen.
It comes from what mysterious land?
With freight of Bagdat or Samarcand?
From under the guns of Arabian forts,
Or out of Al-Raschid's golden ports?
From India, or the barbarous isles
Where the Pacific summer smiles?
I envy the sea-bird sailing there
In the trackless ocean of blue air;
It can see and it can hear
What may never meet my eye or ear.

"I look to the east—all things ascend,
And with them the eye and the heart must tend,—
Only the heavy earth opprest,
Turning forever out of the west,
Rolls down and down: the fancy feels
The sinking, and the spirit reels!

What was the east an hour ago
Even while I gaze is no longer so—
I am plunging now through its azure veil,
While another rises dim and pale,
And this must shortly sink afar
To hold in the west the evening-star.

"Here clinging we are daily cast
Into the future, out of the past,—
Through the sunshine into the night,—
Through the darkness into the light.
Thus we whirl in the noiseless stream,
And the sky glides over us like a dream,
Full of stars and mystery
And prophecy of things to be.

"This very moment we hold a place
Never filled before in space—
Where never again the world shall reel—
The same wave never revisits the wheel.

Year by year our course is run
In a voyage around the sun;
In million circlings forth and back
We never retrace a once gone track.
Did the countless earths abroad, like snails,
Leave behind them shining trails,
What a web of strange design
Through the eternal space would shine!
And such a web of marvellous lines
Left by each satellite and sun,
Though by us unseen, still clearly shines
To the observant eye of One.

"And did the countless souls of men
Leave life-trails visible to the ken,
Each hued with colour to betray
The character which passed that way,
How intricate and variously hued
Would seem the woof of pathways rude

Across the world's great surface laid!
And so inwoven with lines of shade,
Of vice and cruelty, anger and hate,
That darkness would preponderate!
And such a woof of tangled trails
Lies o'er the world and never pales—
Never varies. On earth's great page
Each soul records its pilgrimage,
And under the eye of God each shines
As visible in eternal lines,
As on the cliff I see from here
The various strata lines appear.

"Thank Heaven! my path shall no longer run
With the common highways under the sun!
From the ways of men it shall lie apart,
On a new and a separate chart;
No other foot shall e'er intrude
In my skiey holds of solitude.

Henceforth alone I walk afar
In the dream which death shall scarcely mar,
Far above the obtrusive ken
And idle inquiry of men.
Already I can here rehearse
The higher life of the universe,
Commune with those spirits whose white tents
Are never stirred by these elements,
Camped on the dim ethereal fields
With meteor banners and starry shields!

"Henceforth my sole companion shall be
My sorrow embodied; and, hermit-like, we
Will renounce the world and rest at ease,
Content with our own sweet sympathies.
Tell me no more of that larger plan,
The charity for and the faith in man:
I have tried it well, and ever found
The seven sins filling its utmost bound!

And they who live in the world must be
One with the world, or content to see
Their dearest rights and their holiest trust
With heels of steel trampled into the dust!
All this I have suffered, and scarcely restrained
At times the revenge whose swift blow would have
gained
The bad world's respect, and left me exempt
A little from all save my soul's self-contempt.
I was as a weed that is chafed on the beach;
But, Heaven be praised! being thrown out of reach,
I have taken firm root in the cliff, where no more
The billows affright with their roll and their roar.
I have tasted the best which the world can bestow,
But friendship turned bitter—love ended in wo!

"In the school of envy, and malice, and strife,
I have studied and learned the lesson of life;
Studied it well from that dreary hour
When the dark-hearted Fates had power,

Ministering at my birth — who threw
Upon my brow their black baptismal dew!
From that sad night what time my spirit's bark,
Sailing over the sea of space,
In a moment ominous and dark,
Was stranded on this desert place,—
This treacherous reef of time,
This rank and poisonous clime
Called earth, where savage men
In hut or palace make their hateful den,—
I have known little peace and less of joy!
And even when a pleasure-seeking boy,
Unlovely faces with distempered tongue
Were my attendants, and they ever hung
Inseparably about me, like the shades
From a baleful torchlight flung,
Which the torch-bearer not evades
Until the light be drenched,
And in the oblivious sea of death and darkness
quenched.

And I have borne this torch—
This flickering life—and still must bear,
Watching it flaunt and flare,
Where all my hopes, like night-moths, fly and scorch
Their airy pinions, till their writhing forms
Drop round my feet a mass of wingless worms!

"But, lo! the tempest of the world is past!
Its passion-bolts are no longer cast
About me, and I feel as one
Who stands to gaze when life is done!
Even the peasant with her bright blue eye
Seemed but the remnant of a cloud gone by;
Or rather let me deem her form
The farewell rainbow of the storm.
I am glad that in leaving this gallery
Of horrors that have frowned on me,
A living thing so pure and bright
Should have closed the hateful place from sight.

"How sweet it is to find release
In this aerial tower of peace!
In this antechamber of the sky
Next to the halls of eternity—
With only one thin door between
This and the outer world serene,
Waiting to take that one step more
When opens the celestial door,
And then, with the sudden splendour blind,
Hear the great portals close behind!"

III.

'TWAS evening, and he mounted high
Up to the terrace that faced the sky.
The fisherman, in his boat below
Swinging to the billows' flow,
Beheld him like a guard of old
On a dusky tower—a shadow bold
Standing against the sundown gold.

There Roland watched the dome of day
In a conflagration fall away,
And saw the first white star that sped
To gaze at the sunset ere it fled.
Westward he saw the spires and domes
Overtopping the noisy homes
Of toil and trade, but all so far
He felt no tremor of the jar

That like a daily earthquake rolls
Through the world of dust-bound souls.

Out of the east the moon arose
Red as Mont Blanc at morning glows;
Over the sea, like a ship on fire,
She sailed with her one star sailing by her.
Long, long he gazed, till he felt the might
And glory that pervade the night.

Awhile he looked upon the seas,
Then gazed to the shadowy orchard trees,
And saw the fisherman's quiet home
Sitting under the vernal dome
Of one great elm, where the fireflies played
With their feast of lanterns nightly made.

He saw the various shadows pass
Over the illumined glass,—

Saw tapers, moving to and fro,
From window to window come and go,
Like those lights which phantom hands
Wave at night o'er marshy lands,—
Saw the maid at her casement lean,
And her shade steal into the night serene.
"Thus from the casements of life," he mused,
"Our shadows are outward cast, confused
Into a greater shade. What eye
Shall trace these phantoms where they fly?
None:—And it much behooves us all
That the lights from whence these shadows fall
Should be guarded well and trimmed with care,
That the flame shall neither sink nor flare,
Protected from the fitful gusts
Blown from the lips of Caliban lusts."

Here and there a meteor fleet,
Struck from the invisible feet

Of Night's wild coursers, fierce and black,
Streamed over the star-paven track:
Or it may be this voiceless leven,
Launched from the unseen clouds of heaven,
Are bolts by spirit-tempests hurled
Into a purgatorial world
Or they may be in the fields of blue
Offsprings of nameless damps and dew,—
Celestial will-o'-wisps at play,
Leading benighted souls astray.

Midnight was near. With a look divine
He saw the maid at her chamber shrine.
Two little tapers with flaming wicks
Burned beside a crucifix.
And while she prayed, it seemed
Over her face a splendour beamed,—
A light of purity and grace
Shed from the suffering Saviour's face.

Her angel look was upward turned;
Her white breast heaved as if it yearned
To breathe her very soul away
In a prayer which words had failed to say.
Her upturned face — her fallen hair,
Her hands clasped on her bosom fair,
Her heaving breast but half concealed,
The fulness of her prayer revealed.

As the watcher gazed, he felt his brain
Branded with a forgotten pain;
And thoughts he had deemed frozen, dead,
Warmed snakelike, by his heart's flame fed,
Till thus the voice of a demon guest
With scornful laugh its joy expressed: —
" *The hawk looks down on the ring-dove's nest;*
He loves her meek voice and her smooth meek breast!
And the beautiful bird shall still be as meek
When her red heart quivers in the falcon's beak!"

"Horrible fiend!" he cried, in pain,
"Back to your baneful den again!
Oh, Death, stand by me in this hour,
And strike me ere the fiend have power!
Have I not, with a terrible oath,
On the breast of the dying sworn my troth?
Did I not swear when Death was at strife,
In the white dome of her bosom, with life,—
Though I had wronged her living trust,—
To be true, ay, as true as the tomb to her dust?
For this she forgave the great wrong I had wrought,
And mingled my name in her last sweet thought,
And promised that, in an hour of fear,
Her soul should be as a guardian near!"

As he spoke, the great tears swam over his gaze,
Till the white moon reeled in delirious haze,
And the stars were unsteady as gust-winnowed chaff—
Still his innermost soul heard the mad demon laugh.

"Look! look again!" Thus cried the fiend,
"One look before the vision is screened—
Oh, never was Parian so fair to the sight!
Oh, never such beauty pulsed love through the night!"

But still the pale man, like some martyr who dies,
Looked into the sky with fixed agonized eyes,
Sighing, "Ida! dear Ida! The hour of fear,
Like a tiger in wait for its prey, crouches here!
I see its red eyes and I feel its hot breath!—
Come forth, thou sweet friend, from the gateways of
Death!
Press me close—side to side—soul to soul—mind
to mind—
Or lead through that path thou too early didst find!"

As he spoke, soft lips, like sunshine warm,
Kissed from his brow the late alarm—
Pale delicate arms his neck caressed,
And the head of a spirit was laid on his breast!

The silken hair that fell unfurled
Still gleamed with the hue of another world:
So soft were her tresses, each breath of the gale
Caressed them in air like a gossamer veil;
And her garments still breathed of ethereal dew
In fields where no mortal has ever passed through.

Then the fiend exclaimed with louder jeers—
While the spirit pressed her hands to her ears,
And gazed with that imploring look
Which only a demon's eye could brook—
"This hour, thou wretched ghost! is thine—
But the next and the next shall all be mine!
The cup is brewing which he shall quaff,
While the angels shall weep and the fiends shall
laugh!
Then thou shalt be scourged away with scorn
Into the outer dark forlorn,
And a mortal head usurp the breast
Which late thy phantom cheek has prest!

Blood warms to blood — dust cleaves to dust —
And in that hour depart thou must,
Thou dead leaf on a midnight gust!"

Then even as a pale dead leaf
Still clinging where its hour is brief,
The spirit-lady in her grief
Shuddered and sighed, as if even now
The wind was plucking her from the bough.

"O Roland!" she cried, "there's one hour of dread,
Blackening like that cloud o'erhead;
A bitter wind is rising fast,
Like this which brings the ocean blast!"
"It shall not be!" the bold man cried;
"No wind shall bear thee from my side!
Let us descend to the altar shrine,
And kneel before the cross divine.
'Tis an altar by repentance built,
In memory of my former guilt,

That a daily prayer might there be made,
To ransom thy departed shade."

Then they descended. The east winds came,
Trampling the sea into phosphor flame,
Which filled the black arch of the night
With sheeted flashings of spectral light.
And every maniac ocean-gust
Scattered the feathery foam, like dust,
Into the air—again and again
Flinging on the window pane
White briny flakes, in rage and spite,
As if to drown the altar light.

IV.

STILL leaning on her lover's breast,
The spirit thus her crime confessed:—

"O Roland! from too much loving thee,
From fear thou wert not wholly mine,
My lips partook of misery,
And left for thee that bitter wine
Pressed in the dark from wo's black vine!

"I drained the cup that kills with sleep,
And pillowed my head on the breast of Death:
He closed the lids that ceased to weep,
And kissed the lips at their latest breath!
That moment I had untimely birth
Out of the chrysalis of earth!

Then I saw that by the horrible deed
The chain was sundered, yet I was not freed;
I had burst away from a windowed cell
Into a dungeon unfathomable—
Into utter night—where I could only hear
The sighing of cold phantoms near!
I shrank with dread; but soon I knew
They also shrank with dread from me;
And presently I began to see
Thin shapes of such a ghastly hue
That sudden agues thrilled me through!

"Some bore in their hands, as sign of guilt,
Keen poinards crimson to the hilt,
Which, ever and anon, in wild despair
They struck into their breasts of air:
Some pressed to their pale lips empty vials
Till frenzied with their fruitless trials:
Some with their faces to the sky,
Walked ever searching for a beam:

Some leaped from shadowy turrets high,
And fell, as in a nightmare dream,
Halfway, and stopped, as some mad rill,
That leaps from the top of an alpine hill,
Ere it reaches the rocks it hoped to win,
Is borne away in a vapour thin:
Some plunged them into counterfeit pools—
Into water that neither drowns nor cools
The horrible fever that burns the brain,
Then climbed despairing to plunge again:
And there were lovers together clasped,
O'er fumeless brazures, who sighed and gasped,
Staring wonder in each other's eye,
And tantalized that they did not die.

"Then as I passed, with marvelling stare
They gazed, forgetting their own despair.
Oh, horrible! their eyes did gloat
Upon me, till at my ashen throat

I felt the fiery viper thirst
Which ever in that dry air is nurst.
And ere I was aware
I had raised the cup it was mine to bear:
My pale lips cleaved to the goblet dim,
And found but dust on the heated rim;
And then I knew—oh, misery!—
It was the same I had pledged to thee—
To absent thee, and to present Death,
Pledged and drained at one long-drawn breath—
Drained to the dregs! Then a hot wind sighed
Close in my ear—"THOU SUICIDE!"
And those two words flew
Into my heart, and pierced it through;
And my eyes grew blind with pain
As a serpent which, with rage insane,
Strikes himself with venomed fangs,
And writhes in the dust with self-dealt pangs.—
Then in my agony's wild excess
I partly swooned, and the pain grew less;

While a form, not all devoid of kindness,
Seemed leaning o'er me in my blindness;
And whispered in my aching ear
Words which then were sweet to hear.

"'Hast thou no friend?' the spirit said,
'Who would rejoice wert thou not dead?
Who in his heart would call thee back
Into the world's green, visible track?
If such an one there be,
Whose soul yearns constantly for thee,
Hearken, and when his voice is heard
Breathing one recalling word,
Arise and hasten, the veil is then
Lifted, and thou mayst return again!
And it shall be thy fate, perchance,
To see the long dull years advance,
And still a bloodless ghost to be
For many a weary century,

When all whom thou hast loved are fled
Into the regions overhead.
Then drearier far that world will be,
With its homes and haunts reminding thee
Of the loved and lost, than even this,
Where the vampire Pain enthronéd is.
But be thou ever wary and wise,
Gazing with unsleeping eyes,
And thou, perchance, shalt find ere long
Some spirit, racked with sin or wrong,
A-weary of Life's daily goad
And sinking under her dusty load,
Who, with rash and desperate hand,
Is about to sever the mortal band
Which binds her down, as once didst thou,
To be the shadow which thou art now.
At such an hour be thou then near,
And when the spirit shall disappear,
And the deserted form
Lies beside thee, silent, warm,

Like a suit of mail in hot disdain
Discarded on a battle plain;
Don thou that heated armour then,
And strive with the striving world again!
And through long struggling it may be,
Thou mayst regain thy liberty!'

"Thus spake the spirit. Then it seemed
A sudden light within me beamed;
And I arose and earthward sped
With a cautious, noiseless tread,
Hearkening ever for that voice
To make my phantom heart rejoice.

"Through fields of twilight first I passed,
Then through a sunset—till at last
I heard the roar
Of ocean jargoning with the shore,—
The sea-like voice of Humanity,
And the tongue-like shouting of the sea!

Then as the night's wide track
Under my feet rolled dim and black,
I heard the voice which summoned me,
'Ida!' it cried, and I came to thee!"

V.

Who that has heard the billows roar
On the rocky bastions of the shore,
Could restrain the sense of sublimity
Which drew him to overlook the sea—
One sea with the terror of many seas!
And held him with the mysterious law
Of wonder and soul-pervading awe,
And sympathy, the child of these?

Out to the foamy balcony,
Where the phosphor light
And the black of the night
Struggled in gloomy rivalry,
Strode Roland—his cloak and hair
Twitched by the briny hands of air,

And all his dusk garb instantly
Made white with the insult of the sea!

Burning through the eastern dark,
At the bow of a perilous bark,
Rising with alternate leap
Out of the valleys of the deep,
He beheld a crimson light
Driving shoreward through the night,—
Watched it as the lurid flame
Straight to its destruction came!
On it drove before the gale,
With empty mast or shivered sail;
And Roland shuddered in his fear
As he saw it neither tack nor veer,
And trembled to think of a crowded deck
Dashed at his feet a shapeless wreck!

A shock! A shriek! The light was drowned!
And the billows leaped with a higher bound!

And the skyward spray the instant after
Was stunned with the ocean's scornful laughter!

Then, bewildered with pain and fright,
Roland descended the stormy height,
Finding his way by the phosphor light,
To seek amid the wild uproar
The drowning bodies thrown on shore.
Suddenly at his feet a form
Lay like an offering from the storm!
White as a stranded wreath of foam,
White as a ghost from its charnel home,
It lay where the gust with blinding flight
Strove to hide the thing from sight,
Like a maniac murderer, to and fro
Raving and flinging the scattering snow
Over the victim that mocks his despair
With its unveiled face and tell-tale stare!
A moment the brave man's heart recoiled,
Then he lifted the body and upward toiled.

VI.

IT was a sight both wild and dread
To see the living for the dead—
One stubborn and unaided form—
Battling with an ocean storm,—
Toiling up the jagged path,
Chased by the billows in their wrath,
Bearing the dripping shape away
Which the sea had deemed its prey.

Thus laden, Roland among the rocks
Strove upward mid the desperate shocks
Of gust and foam—climbing a track
As crooked as that on the tempest's wrack,
Where the armèd Thunder in his ire
Descends in a zigzag path of fire!

The long black hair
Of the drownéd form he strove to bear,
Flashed abroad on the wet sea air,
Wild as the tresses of Despair:
And he thought, as he gazed on the drooping head
Where the writhing locks were so wildly spread,
Of the twisted horrors Medusa wore—
And a shudder pierced him to the core.

But now he heard, or deemed he heard,
The sound of that most piteous word,
That only word the full heart knows
To syllable its joys and woes,—
A sigh! Like a night-bird sweeping near,
Its soft wing fluttered past his ear,
And he felt the heave of the rounded breast
Which close against his own was prest:
Then through his frame he took new strength,
And with upward toiling gained at length

The gusty height! A moment there,
While the lightning lent its sheeted glare,
That group stood in the misty air
Like statues on a terrace high,
Relieved on a dusky wall of sky.

VII.

INTO the care of a gray-haired crone,
The sybil who tended his dull hearth-stone,
He yielded the body. A couch was spread,
And the lady was laid as she were not dead;
And the dame from off the swooning face
Smoothed the wet locks into their place;
And Roland, when the salt sea-spray
Which blurred his vision was cleared away,
Holding a white torch, bent to trace
The features of that sleeping face.
His heart stood still!
His blood ran chill!
His wide eyes could not gaze their fill!
And as his marvelling face was drawn
Nearer and nearer to stare thereon —

Slowly—slowly as a veil
Lifted from a phantom's visage pale,
The lady's delicate lids were raised,
And in Roland's face the soft orbs gazed
With all that touching tenderness
Which only loving eyes express.

He had clasped the ghost of his beloved,
And not a tremor in his soul was moved,—
From lips of air had taken the kiss
With not a fear to mar the bliss,—
And heard what the threatening demon said,
With a pang of pain but not of dread!

But now an icy horror stole
Through the deepest depths of his inmost soul;
For here indeed was the risen dead
For whom the funeral tears were shed!
A spectre of dust!—a ghost of clay!—
That lived when the spirit had passed away.

He trembled, but could not move or speak:
He had gazed in those eyes till his will was weak.

Then the lady sighed, and her bosom heaved,
And she faintly smiled as her heart was grieved;
While the thought of pain which shadowed her brow
Said, "Roland, ah! Roland, thou lovest me not
now!"
Then a great tear stole from under her lid,
And rebukingly over her white cheek slid:
Then Roland cried as he clasped her hand,
"'Tis a dream that I cannot understand!
Forgive me, dear Ida, if even I seem
To wrong thy sweet shade in the dark of a dream!"

"Oh, joy! Thou hast called me 'dear Ida,'" she cried,
And she lovingly drew him more close to her side.
That voice—'twas the same he had heard in gone
days,
While she poured in his eyes as of old her soft gaze.

Then she sighed—"Ah! dear Roland, a vision it
seems?—
To me 'tis the sweetest of all waking dreams!
And let me recount in this hour of bliss
How I fled out of the past into this,
Escaping from Death's black precipice."

VIII.

"Far back in that dark desperate hour,
When the swart mandragore had power,—
While the suicidal draught, like flame,
Through all the galleries of my frame
Spread its malignant fire—even then
I repented and prayed for life again—
Not from the torture; but that I knew,
When it seemed too late, that thou wert true.

"And then I swooned, and heard the tread
Of muffled feet—while sad hearts said,
In sighs and whispers—'She is dead! is dead!'
And then I knew,—oh, wo was me!—
That word was a shaft of pain to thee,

A shaft which I had winged with flame
And sped—and yet could not reclaim!
I saw thy high soul with the blow
Struck to the dreary plains of wo,
Yet struggling in its fall, as when
An eagle, sailing with sunward ken,
Receives from the heartless archer's bow
The envious arrow winged from below.

"Then I felt thy hasty farewell kiss,—
A touch of mingled torture and bliss;
And my soul within me writhed with pain
That I could not return that kiss again.
And then you fled! I heard the door
Swing loud behind—and heard no more.
My very soul then swooned—and all
Was blacker than midnight's starless pall.
And more I know not—till a long cool breath
Came into my breast and chased out Death—
Or that dark sleep which did counterfeit

Black Death so well, that I scarcely yet
Can realize the miracle
Which finds me freed from his dreamless spell.

"Then I awoke and saw the room
Tricked out with all the pompous gloom
Of funeral weeds—the air was sick
With incense fumes suspended thick
And blue, as at morn o'er a stagnant lake
Swings the venomous mist ere the winds awake.
There I saw two tapers with fiendish glare
Burning in the ghastly air;
And my breast with horrible pain was weighed,
As if by the weight of a black dream made.
I found it was a cross of gold
Which lay on my bosom so heavy and cold—
A cross entwined with lily-bells,
And framed in a wreath of immortelles.
A garland of flame—a cross of fire—
And I outstretched on a martyr's pyre

Had been less terrible!—So at last,
By struggling I grew strong, and cast
These emblems of death from off my breast,
And, breathing, felt no more opprest.

"Then you should have heard the shriek
Of Death's stout wardress!—Pale and weak,
She reeled and tottered beyond the door,
And fell in a fit on the marble floor.
She awoke a maniac—her hair turned gray—
And a maniac she goes to this very day.

"Then the household and the priest came in—
The priest in his robe as black as sin!—
All shuddered and shrank; till I rose and smiled,
When they rushed to my side with wonder wild,
And cried, in their mingled joy and dread—
'She lives! Our Ida is not dead!'

IX.

"Days past, and daily I asked for thee,
Till at last they pointed over the sea,
And said, in the madness of thy despair
Thy bark had followed the red sun there.
For hours they had watched the westward sail
Growing in the distance pale,
And sinking till beyond the line
Of the flaming, sunset-gilded brine
It set, like a star,—and never more
Came tidings of that bark to shore.

"Then with a grief too great for speech,
I wandered daily to the beach

With one companion gray and old,
A reverend friar—who hourly told
His '*Aves*' as we walked the sand—
And the pious tears, on his sunbrown hand
His old eyes dropped, outcounted the beads
As he thought of my sorrow! My poor heart
bleeds
That these tearful eyes shall no more win
A sight of that saintly Capuchin!

"At last we found
A little shallop westward bound;
The daintiest thing that ever yet
Was on the treacherous ocean set.
Under the prow we read her name
Written in ciphers of golden flame,—
'THE FIRE BEARER.' Each letter did make,
The semblance of a twisted snake,—
One with the other all intervolved,
Like a riddle that is slowly solved.

"What ails the dame? What thus can make
Her eyes so wide and her limbs to quake?"
The crone replied, with a look of awe,
"Forgive me, lady, I thought I saw—
My sight is dim,—
'Twas a foolish whim,—
But I thought I saw a fiery snake,
A little streak of flame just there
Writhing through your tangled hair!"
The lady smiled, and gathered in
Her tresses betwixt her breast and chin;
And thus pursued the delirious theme,
While Roland listened like one in a dream.

"So near the shallop tacked and sailed,
That in a desperate moment I hailed
The skipper, who leaned against the helm,
Looking the lord of the watery realm.
Round went the rudder,—the sail went round;
And the light bark neared like a leaping hound;

Then, seeing what I had done, I sunk
And swooned on the breast of the dear old monk!

"Then, half-awaking, I felt the motion
Beneath me of a summer ocean,
And dimly heard a voice of glee
Singing some ballad about the sea!—
'Twas the skipper's voice, as the helm he prest,
Heading the shallop out to the west!

"The Capuchin was at my side,
Or else for very fear I had died.
There we sat on deck, in the breezy shade
By the one tall lateen canvas made,—
Still flashing on in our track of foam
When the venturous sea-gull turned for home.

"Thus dreamily sitting, for many a day
Under the bow we heard the spray,

And watched our backward path of white,
And gazed on its liquid fire by night.

"Under us eastward the sea went by,
Over us westward went the sky—
The sun and the moon and those silver barks,
Those soul-freighted celestial arks,
The starry fleets of the shoreless night,
Were the only things that surpassed our flight!
As a swallow chases the summer, we sped,
Chasing the days that before us fled."

X.

"THEN came the calm—we called it so—
But the skipper knew, as now we know,
That it was only the hungry Storm,
Crouching back with his awful form,
The better that he might spring and light
Down on the unsuspecting night!

"The sail was furled,—the hatch made fast,—
And the friar and I sat close to the mast.
Then came the dark and the roaring gale,
And we sailed as an autumn leaf might sail,
Blown by a loud-tornado gust—
And the spray was like a blinding dust.

"Then to the shivering mast we clung
Still closer—while the friar's tongue

Over his *paternosters* ran
As only a pious friar's can;
And my trembling lips, again and again,
Strove vainly to respond 'amen.'

"The hard old skipper laughed outright
To behold us clinging to the mast in fright.
Then suddenly he cried—'land! ho!'
And we saw in the west the crimson glow
Of a lighthouse—or what we deemed was so!

"Fiercer and fiercer the loud gale came,
Driving us onward towards the flame.
The skipper strove to change our course,
Pressing the helm with giant force:—
Battling a moment 'twixt rudder and gale,
The light ark shuddered like a veering sail—
Then a crash!—and a curse!—o'er the stern of
the bark
The helm and the helmsman plunged into the dark!

And the shallop leaped forth to the black unknown,
With the joy of a steed when his rider is thrown!
Spurning the waves and the wind's control,
On, on it sped to its direful goal!
I hid my face in the old man's breast:
And then—and then—you know the rest!

"Oh, Roland, a fearful dream was mine—
Those swooning moments among the brine!
I saw thee stand in a midnight tower,
And a beautiful fiend had thee in her power.
I saw her pale lips pressed to thine;
I saw ye kneel at an altar-shrine;
And then I heard your mingled prayer,
That, like a raven croaking in air,
Hung black and ominous, but did not soar!
And then you named her by my name,
And that hot word clung to my heart like flame
Slung from a torch! And I heard no more!

"Oh, Roland, wherefore tremble so?
Or wherefore stoops your brow so low?
Oh, dreary hour! oh, wo is me!
If this terrible dream should prove to be
The shadow of mad reality!
Look up, and assure me it is not so—
Or let me die with the sudden blow
Of the horrible truth! At thy command
Death shall strike with most welcome hand.

"Oh, wo is me! Oh, wo is me!
Would I were lying under the sea!
Or would that dear old friend were here
Who sleeps so low on his briny bier,
To mount with thee to that sinful place
To meet the demon face to face;
With exorcism and with prayer
To scourge her into the utmost air!

XI.

Was it the sound of a human cry,
Or wail of a night-bird driven by?
The lady started and halfway rose,
With that look the walking sleeper shows,—
With large eyes staring vacantly,
That seem to listen and not to see.
Then, with a tongue of pitiful glee,
She cried, "O Roland, if that should be
The voice of my friend so old and gray,
Struggling among the rocks and spray!

"There, did you not hear? that wild cry through the roar!
Hark again! It is his! Wave the torch at the door,

And beacon him in! Oh, I faint as I think,
Perchance how he clings to some terrible brink!"
Even while she spoke, as if at her will,
The door swung wide, and over the sill
The gust and the roar and the spray swept in,
Like a crew of wild pirates, with insolent din;
And suddenly a group of three
Toiled breathlessly after, all dripping the sea.

There came the monk in his robe of brown,
Over his breast his white beard blown
And sparkling like a gust of foam;
As if old Neptune should leave his home,
To traverse the dry land up and down
Disguised in a friar's hood and gown.

And bearing a lantern, so covered with spray
That the light could scarcely emit a ray,
Came the fisherman, whose sturdy arm
Had rescued the pious man from harm.

There, too, was the maiden, the fisherman's child,
With her glowing cheeks and eyelids mild.
For many a mile about the coast,
That father and child were the country's boast.
And many a sailor on a far-off deck
Remembered Agatha and the wreck.
Fame fondly pictured their struggling forms
Battling against the blackest storms.
Through day or dark they might be found
Braving the tempest in their round;
And thus to-night they had met the storm,
And rescued from death this saintly form.

That moment there
Was a living picture bold and rare,
With its massive lights and shadows thrown
From the torch in the hands of the withered crone,
Exalted above her own wild hair
Which streamed like the shreds of a banner in air,

Tattered, confused, as if torn in the strife
Of the seventy years' war waged by Death against Life.

The lady arose with joy and ran
And fell on the breast of the ancient man;
And wept such tears as a child might shed
On the breast of a parent just saved from the dead.
Then from her heart of gratitude
She thanked the fisherman, where he stood
Gazing on her with marvelling face,
As if in some enchanted place
He stood, with uncontrolled sight,
Chained to a vision of delight.

And then she seized the daughter's hand:
A moment her large eyes softly scanned
The modest maid, with look as mild
As a mother casts on her beauteous child,
Conscious that its face confers
A ray of splendour back to hers.

Then drawing her near with a smile of bliss,
Pronounced her thanks in a tender kiss.
Suddenly pale grew the maiden's lips,
And her soul was veiled with a deep eclipse;
And she sunk at the old monk's feet with dread,
Begging his blessing to rest on her head.
And cried, "Oh, let me see and touch
The CROSS, which we cannot kiss too much!
And count one prayer on the beads divine!"
And the old monk murmured,—"My blessing is
thine."
While he laid his hand on her shining hair;
But it seemed like a fiery gauntlet there!

Then tracing his girdle and fumbling his dress,
He cried, with a visage of deep distress,
"Oh, wo is me! They are lost in the sea—
That miracle cross and rosary!
Torn from my side in those desperate shocks
When the billows were lifting me over the rocks.

Oh, wo is me! They were made from a tree
In the garden of holy Geth——"
Here the sea,
Through the open door, hurled into the place
Such a cloud of spray that the old man's face
Was smothered with brine. The white torch hissed,
And all the room was blind with the mist.

Then thrice the maiden, with look distressed,
Signed the cross on her brow and breast,
And thus to the friar her fear confessed:—
"I feel in my soul what I cannot say;
But something so wicked has blown this way,
That I cannot choose but shudder and shrink,
As if I were dragged to a horrible brink.
A demon is breathing this very air,
Which can only be banished afar with prayer!"

The monk bent soothingly over her form,
And said, "Be calm, my child, it is only the storm;

Take cheer, take cheer!
It is only the loud wind shrieking near.
The wind and the night and the sea.
Are all that be
Abroad to fill the soul with fear."

XII.

THE lady, who heard what the maiden had said,
As dizzy with pain, clasped her hands to her head;
While her white bosom heaved as with heart-broken
sighs,
And she turned upon Roland her pitiful eyes;
And he read in her visage of pallid dismay,
Far more than her language of sorrow could say.

"Oh, the terrible dream! It is true—it is true!
And a beautiful demon there waiteth for you!
For you! Roland, you! and I to be left
In a poisonous world of all comfort bereft!"

"Though I die, it shall vanish!" the desperate man
cried,
"No demon shall hold me away from thy side!"
The torch halfway dwindled—the crone muttered
and moaned—
The maid hid her face and her deep bosom groaned!
Then seizing the monk, like one in despair,
Roland led through the hall to the shadowy stair;
And said, while ascending, "Let thy holy words be
A scourge which shall drive this fiend into the sea!
Ay, into its own native sea of black pain,
So deep it shall never turn earthward again!"

Then the monk's pious pleasure burst to laughter
aloud,
Like a hot gust that blows the red leaves in a
cloud;
And he cried—"By the Pope, whose brown livery
I wear,
It shall frighten the night with its shriek of despair!

And when *my* Pope hears the good deed I have done,
He will call me to kneel at his great crimson throne;
And knowing the height of all priestly desire,
He will crown this old brow with the sacred attire
Of a cardinal's hat—flaming scarlet as fire!

"No monarch is half so sublime as our Pope!
You will visit our Rome and behold him, I hope;—
You will find him enthroned in magnificent state,—
His brow overweighed with the burthensome weight
Of care for the souls of mankind! You will see
The great of all nations there bending the knee—
Proud kings and their courts in their splendour replete,
Like an ocean of flame, surging up to his feet;—
All so eagerly crowding to press on his shoe
The kiss of allegiance, that the place through and through
Grows oppressively heated—besides, as you know,
Our Rome's a warm climate—excessively so!

"You will probably go there in carnival time,—
And see what no pencil, however sublime,
Could picture with justice. If one did not know
That the thing was a sanctioned and sanctified show,
One might deem he had passed into Lucifer's regions,
And think he saw Hell pouring out its red legions!
Indeed, they *do* say, that beneath his black dome
The Devil *does* try to imitate Rome!
But this is rank scandal—you see what I mean—
In no place but Rome can you find such a scene.

"And then, oh! those gorgeous great festival nights,
When the huge dusky dome is one fabric of lights,
Done with marvellous skill, which naught baffles or mars,—
A temple of flame!—a mosaic of stars!

"Believe me, nowhere are such fireworks known,
As you'll find in our Rome. Quite distinct and alone
They stand; for the artist who plans them is one
In that line of business not easily outdone!"

XIII.

THEY gained the gusty balcony
Where the light from the chamber streamed out to the sea.
What ailed the friar that he seemed to fail
And grasped for support on the shadowy rail?
Why did he shiver and seem so faint?
Was it that, like a beautiful saint,
He beheld the spirit-lady kneeling
With mild eyes full of tears and feeling,
Clasping on her bosom fair
The crucifix, which piously there
Rose and fell on the tide of prayer?

"I am very old and nigh to death,
And climbing that stairway has taken my breath!"
He murmured at last:—"Ah, me! ah, me!
I am very weak from the abuse of the sea!
And the chilly wet is piercing me through
As if I had slept in a poisonous dew,
And awoke with all the horrible pains
Which death can inflict with chills and blains!

"It will pass anon:—meantime do thou
Secure the precious moment now—
Go seize on that polluted cross,
And into the sea, with a curse and a toss,
Fling it afar, as you would fling
Some black, dead offensive thing,
Hurled away with fierce disdain,
Never to be reclaimed again!
And then—and then—oh! this terrible chill,
Piercing me like an electric thrill

In a cavern of ice!—The punishing ire
Of—our abbot, though wielding great lashes of fire,
Were easier to bear than this shiver intense,
Like icicles piercing the innermost sense!
Then take thou this girdle, which grasp like a
scourge,
And wield through the room!—It hath power to
purge
The air from such envious spirits as this,
Who would rob even hell of its last ray of bliss!"

Then Roland, with averted head,
Strode in and did as the friar said;
He seized the cross—through the open door
It spun to the dark and the wild uproar!

The spirit arose with a shriek of wo,
Crying, "This is the storm! It must be so!
The same I foretold thee an hour ago!

Though thou comest, O Roland! as one in swift ire,
And armed with those red hissing scourges of fire:
Oh! know, Roland, know that the fiends of the pit,
The Arachnes of wo, are all weaving their wit
In webs to ensnare thee! Already thy will
Is tangled, confused in the threads of their skill:
Ere thou strike I depart—yet again and again
My hand shall be laid on thy forehead of pain.
And when thou hast passed through this fiery test,
When reason and calm have re-entered thy breast,
Again will I sit by thy side, and renew
The chain which the demons have sundered in
two."

Ere the red scourge was lifted, the spirit had flown
With a sigh in the air, and then followed a groan,
And Roland dropt down with the weight of a stone.
And the monk, leaning o'er him, breathed into his ear
Thoughts without words, which his spirit in fear

Beheld as black tangible visions at strife,
Struggling which should be foremost to poison his life.

Down in the shadowy hall below,
The maid and the fisher were turning to go,
When the lady with a mild command,
With language sweet and countenance bland,
Recalled the maiden, and seizing her hand,
Pressed it to her bosom white
And cold as a marble tomb at night;
And murmured in accents sweet and mild—
"We must be friends—dear friends—my child!
And in token of this, this little ring,
Quite a simple yet sacred thing,
I place on your finger. It is, you see,
The emblem of *wisdom* and *eternity;*
And a symbol of what our love must be—
Wise, watchful, unending—that hereafter we,

Even in a future clime,
May look backward to the realms of time,
And say it was upon that night
When the heavens were black and the seas were
        white,
We plighted the faith that shall never grow cold,
And linked our two souls with this serpent of gold!"

Part Second.

I.

WANDERING over the summer plain,
Like one gone, for love, insane,
And gathering through field and lane,
Those wild blooms whose breath is bane,
Passed Agatha, her golden hair
More golden in the noonday air,
Fluttering free from the wonted braid
Which her hand no longer made;
But twined with such wild vines and weeds
As the rank marsh and woodland breeds:
And like pale Autumn, when she grieves,
Her brow was bound with crimson leaves

Plucked from the woodbine, and her breast
In a scarf of withered vines was drest;
Her cheeks were white, her eyes were bright,
And full of supernatural light.

Oh, Heaven! it is a sight to make
The heart of the stoutest stoic ache,
To see a maid so young and fair
Decked in the garments of despair!
Like a statued sorrow, overrun
With garlands yellowing in the sun.

And thus as she gathered the leaves and flowers,
Fit only to deck the forbidden bowers
Wherein some pale enchantress fiend
In noxious odours is veiled and screened,
She murmured her fancies as they came
Out of her brain like wings of flame:—

"They are gone, all the blooms by the wild April strown
In the pathway of May;
For the passionate breath of the Summer has blown
Their leaves to decay.

"And the flowers of childhood must wither and fall,
And pine unto death,
When the summer of passion breathes over them all
Its feverish breath.

"Where the violets out from the green hedges stole,
Unnoticed to shine,
The poppy is waving its fiery bowl,
A bowl of red wine.

"These goblets of crimson, these beakers of sleep,
Each a chalice of flame,
I will pluck for my lady, her soul they shall steep
In desires without name.

"And the berries that burn on the poisonous vine,
Like embers blown red,
I will gather and string, and gayly entwine
Round her beautiful head.

"From this wild ivy-climber, that strangles the tree
And robs it of green,
I will weave for my lady a garland, and she
Shall be crowned like a queen.

"Once I knew where to find the most beautiful blooms
When the year was at noon,
Those delicate spirits called out of their tombs
By the trumpet of June:—

"Now the daisies and buttercups fade at my touch—
And even the sweet-brier,
That wild parent of roses my heart loved so much,

Now wilts in my hand as if held in the clutch
Of fingers of fire.

"Oh, this beautiful ring! and this gem in its head
So scarlet and bright!
I feel a soft warmth through my quick pulses shed
With a sense of delight!
Like a spark caught from Mars, as lovely and red
It burns in the night!

"Since I knew the fair donor, a wonderful change
Has mantled the earth;
The summer goes by, and no longer I range
Through its bowers of mirth.

"The birds have grown hateful that sing in the light;
No longer I hark
To any save those which talk madness all night
To the fiery-eyed dark!

"Thou gem, let me press thee again and again
With a passionate kiss!
Oh! a pleasure inflames me that almost is pain,
The pain of pure bliss!"

II.

LIKE a shell among the rocks,
A tempest-stranded nautilus,
Wrecked but not ruined by the shocks—
Lifted and lodged from danger—thus
The dainty bark was found,
Sitting upright, safe and sound,
Like a vessel on the stocks,
Waiting but to feel
The loosening hammers at her keel
To launch upon the sea
And leap away to liberty,
Like a captured swan set free.

Already there were toiling men
Labouring hard at the spars and ropes;
And on the cliff, with anxious ken,
Gazing with mingled fears and hopes,
Stood Roland, with the lady's form
Languidly leaning on his arm.

There, too, with his beard and hair
Swaying to the summer air,
Stood the monk with mutterings low,
That like the billows' mystical speech,
Hissing, murmuring up the beach,
Were poured in such a Babel flow
None knew if they were prayers or no—
Save the lady, who ever and anon
Responded till the monk was done.

Still labouring at the ropes and spars,
Yo-heaving, like a group of tars,

Toiled the men; but the firm-set keel
Clung to the rock like magnet to steel.
Whereat the monk, as if in wrath,
Hurried down the zigzag path.
In the breeze his white beard shook,
Like the foam of a mountain brook.
He laid his shoulder against the keel,
At once she began to stagger and reel.
"Again!" he cried, "and all together!"
And like a steed that has broken its tether,
Away she sped with a bound and a quiver,
Making the cloven water shiver
With the sudden blow! And then she wheeled,
Restively pawing the watery field,
Angered to feel the clinging check
Of the shoreward cable about her neck.

The sea, to one of its slumberous calms,
Now sunk as it never would waken more:

Its breakers were only as flocks of lambs
Bleating and gambolling along the shore,
Where of late the storm-lion insane
Had shaken abroad his tumultuous mane,
Frightening the land with his rage and his roar.
Round the headland to a little bay
They led the shallop and drew it to land,
Till at the golden beach it lay
With its keel on the smooth wet sand.

How haughtily the gilded prow
Lifted its yawning, dragon head!
And backward — shaping the graceful bow —
The dragon's flying wings were spread;
Where its curious name,
In letters of flame,
Burned in ciphers of golden red:
Lo! there she stood, as fresh and staunch
And bright as at her birthday launch.

III.

Out of the great commercial town,
Summoned by the bark's renown,
Came the masters and merchants down,
And crowded the beach;
While with gesture and speech,
With eyes of wide wonder and looks of delight,
They declared such a sight
In the waters of Christendom never was known.

The very dragon seemed to feel
A tremor of pleasure that thrilled to the keel;
And like a lady fair and proud,
Flattered by praises breathed too loud,
The shallop withdrew—so it seemed to the crowd—
And somewhat stiffly its acknowledgment bowed.

But perchance it was only the swell
Of the waters that under her rose and fell.

And there were builders, with rule and line,
Measuring its breadth and length,
Gathering its secret of grace and strength;
While, sitting on the sand,
With accurate and dexterous hand,
An artist secured the fair design.

Singing a scrap of maniac song,
Agatha pressed through the wondering throng,
Bedecked in garlands of strange device,
As if for a heathen sacrifice:
She scattered blossoms from her hand
Around the keel where it pressed the sand,
Until it seemed to be wading through
A flowery foam of various hue,
And singing still, began to deck
The dragon's curved and haughty neck,

Slipping over the glittering head
A garland of yellow, and blue, and red;
And then withdrew a space, to admire
The beautiful collar of floral fire.

When the fisherman saw his child,
And heard her voice so strange and wild,
Over his visage scarred and tanned
The trouble spread. Then he knelt on the sand,
And hiding his face in his sunburnt hand,
He sobbed aloud, while the tears of pain
Through his fingers trickled plain,
And dropt on the thirsty ground like rain.

Along the beach his forsaken net
Lay weltering in the briny wet,
Where the scaly things in their despair
Were struggling in their tangled snare,
Flashing their silvery sides in air.

Around the shore in the sunshine bright,
Like webs of those invisible looms
Whose noiseless shuttles are plied at night
Among the briers and garden blooms,
Innumerable nets were spread
On stake and fence, and over the head
Of many a low marsh-willow, to dry—
The delight, until now, of the fisherman's eye:
For each, he thought, ere the season was o'er,
With a miraculous draught would come to shore,
And thereby enable him proudly to pay
His daughter's dower on her wedding-day.

But, alas! the wary Fates had cast
Their unseen net in the river of Life;
And all his hopes, the best and last,
Were dragged to land with a fruitless strife,
To pine on the sand without relief,
And die on the sunless shores of grief.

IV.

Down from the height,
With steps as light
As a party for a bridal bedight,
The lady and the monk were seen
Gliding through the pathway green,
While, with uneasy tread
And drooping head,
With one arm at the lady's zone,
And one on the friar's shoulder thrown,
Pale Roland walked between.
They seemed, to a gazer far away,
Like a happy group in the fields of May.

Out of the little belfry near,
A bell, with accents loud and clear,
Poured its pious peal abroad,
To turn the thoughts of men to God.
Far and wide through the valley round
Sailed the silver wings of sound,—
Like a flock of doves rung out,
Wheeling joyfully about,
Flashing from their pinions white
A sense of quiet and delight.

The lady, as before a shrine
Suddenly called to thoughts divine,
Dropt upon her knees straightway,
With hanging head that seemed to pray.
And as one who stumbles with a curse and a groan,
The monk fell in the pathway prone,
And lay, like a statue overthrown;
Muttering harshly to the air
Something that passed for a hurried prayer.

And when the bell was done, he rose
Red in the face as a furnace glows—
And cried, "Now, hang that sacristan!
What pious crank has got into the man,
Thus to be ringing a vesper tune
In the very middle of afternoon?
It takes one down so unawares
That one can scarcely remember his prayers!
And besides, we have an old tradition,
Which may be merely superstition,
That when one kneels and forgets his prayer,
The Devil is also kneeling there!"

The crowd gave way as the party neared:
And much they marvelled at the friar's beard,
Hanging so long with crispy flow,
Like a winter hemlock's barb of snow.
But when with wondering eyes they saw
The lady, they held their breath with awe,

Transfixed and speechless with the sense
Of beauty's rare magnificence.
All bared their brows as she passed between,
Bowing like subjects to a queen.
The monk straightway regained his mood,
And blessed the courteous multitude;
For he thought such deference alone could be
Paid to his age and piety.

When the lady beheld the maid
In her tawdry veil of flowers arrayed,
She pressed her with a warm embrace;
And smoothing the wild locks from her face,
Printed a kiss upon her brow,
Which brought to her forehead the crimson glow,
As if smitten by the sudden blow
Of a fiery hand! Then said, in accents gay,
"Come, my sweet friend, come away,—
You must go with us to-day.

Under the shadowy sail we'll sit,
While our fairy bark shall flit
Like a swallow that stoops to lave
Its burnished bosom in the wave,
Just tipping with its airy breast
The enamoured billow's eager crest!"

Straightway, without more remark,
The jubilant party gained the bark.
Then the monk came to the bow,
And overleaning the dragon prow,
A moment anxiously scanned the crowd,
And cried, in a voice of mirth aloud,
"Who is there here so loves the sea
That he will bear us company?
One who knows the billowy realm,
To trim the sail and to set the helm?
Who will man our little ship
For a three-hours' pleasure trip?"

Up stepped the fisherman; but ere
His feet had touched the slanting plank,
He staggered back, and shuddering sank,
Like one who swoons with sudden fear!
Then shouldering his way till he gained the sand,
A withered sailor, wrinkled and tanned,
Holding a piece of a helm in his hand,
And twitching his waistband with swaggering air,
Cried, "Avast there, my hearty!
While I'm of your party,
You'll scarcely be wanting these land-lubbers there!
Oh, ho! I'll be bound
That you thought I was drowned,
Because I plunged overboard into the dark!
But with this stout piece of helm,
What sea could o'erwhelm
A sailor who fears neither billow nor shark?—
Who on a fragment of wreck
Sits as safe as on deck,
And brings it to shore like a well-guided bark?"

The lady laughed with joy insane
When she beheld the skipper again.
With a bound and a leap, he cleared the side
And strode the deck with his former pride:
Once more he leaned against the helm—
Once more he was lord of the watery realm!

V.

THE cable was loosed—the bark was free,
And like a white sea-bird, it flew to the sea.
Of all the shapes that swim
Through the ether blue and dim,
Or over the swinging ocean skim,
With their lifted plumes for sails
Set before the summer gales—
Or on enchanted lakes the swan,—
Or the swift wind-footed fawn,
None might with that fairy bark compare,
Less in the water than in the air,
As she sped from shore through a track of foam,
With the sudden joy and speed

Of the carrier-bird when its wings are freed
And it darts from its alien tower for home!
Flying away with its white sail full,
It doubled the headland like a gull,
That, careening suddenly, seems to dip
In the flashing brine its white wing's tip.
Then up and down the coast it bore—
In and out, as it would explore
The hundred inlets of the shore!

With all her garments fluttering wild,
On the deck the fisherman's child
Stood by the lady, who proudly sat
On a little throne—where an Indian mat
Mantled the floor, like a flowery moss
Where Mab and her fairies gambol and toss,
And covered with figures of strange device,
And scented with odours of orient spice,
Which rose like an incense heavy and sweet
When the lady stirred her delicate feet.

The maiden stood robbing her own bright hair
To garland the lady's locks less fair:
The scarlet wreath seemed a brighter red
As it gilded the braids of that darker head,—
And the poisonous berries livelier shone
Like crimson embers newly blown.
It seemed a chaplet fit for Fame
To bind on the brazen brow of Shame,
The guerdon of deeds which have no name!—
Like Evening wreathed with sunset flame,
The lady sat; and in her eyes,
Like shadows which the day defies,
Nursed by the darkness, there seemed to rise
Thoughts which on the black wings fly
Of sin-engendered mystery!

Still humming a scrap of maniac tune,
The maiden stood, like frenzied May,
At the close of her last sweet day
Casting all her blossoms away

Into the burning lap of June!
Stripping herself of every flower
She shed them all, a fiery shower,
Over the lady, till she was as bright
As a statue decked with lamps at night,—
Those little lamps of various hue,
Scarlet, purple, green, and blue,
Which in myriads star the dark
In a royal festive park.

Many a venomous brier and burr
Among the rest she gave to her:—
There were slips of hemlock, tips of fir,
Mingled with leaves of juniper;
Monkshood flower and mandragore,
Henbane rank and hellebore,
And nightshade breathing deadly malice;
And there was the foxglove's purple chalice
Full of bane; but which, 'tis said,
Hath power to thrill and move the dead.

And there, like goblets brimming red
Stolen from a demon's palace,
Shone the poppies, flaming bright;
And those which had a withered look
At the lady's touch fresh vigour took,
As if it did their lives renew
With a taste of their own noxious dew;
Even as stars that wilt in the light
Revive again in the lap of Night,—
Thus each, like Mars, refreshed with fire,
Flamed where they lay; while high and higher,
Heaving with a strange desire,
The lady's breast 'gan swell; and she
Kissed the maid with unwonted glee,—
The maid who, without a blossom left,
Looked scarce less lovely thus bereft,—
While the other shone as gorgeous and gay
As if she were decked for a queen of May
In a fiery tropic far away!

VI.

Low at her feet pale Roland sat,
Gazing up in her radiant face;
And said, "In such a time and place
How sweet were song, did thy voice but grace
The air with melody!" Whereat
The crownéd lady smiled, and sent
Her glance to a little instrument
Which a crimson cord made fast
Up at the side of the polished mast;
And without further sign or command,
Roland placed it in her hand.

It was a curious instrument,
A kind of Persian mandolin,

Found perchance in an Arab's tent,
With every manner of gem besprent,
And wrought with all that tracery
Which Eastern art is cunning in:
The body was ribbed like a shell of the sea,
Yet black, and burnished as ebony;
The graceful neck was long and thin,
Where the cords ran up to golden keys;
And it looked as it had only been
Waked to mysterious melodies,
On phantom lakes and enchanted seas,
Flashing to fingers weird and wan,
In the minstrel ages lost and gone.

Waiting to hear the wakened lute,
The very air and the sea hung mute;
And the maiden, breathless with listening desire,
Crouched silently down at the side of the friar.
The lady's fingers, like swift wings,
Over the flashing cordage stirred,

Till music, like an answering bird,
Suddenly leaped from out the strings.
Round and round the cadence flew,
Sailing aloft and dropping low,
Now soaring with the wild sea-mew,
Flushing its breast in the sunset glow,
Then slowly dropping down the air,
Wailing with a wild despair,
Down and down,
Till it seemed to drown,
With wide pinions on the brine,
Weltering with no living sign,
Till the listener's pitying eye
Wept that so fair a thing should die.
Then with malicious laughter loud,
Jeering the sighing hearer's grief,
In a moment wild and brief,
Filling the air with mockery,
It leapt to the sky and pierced the cloud,
Soaring and soaring, till it seemed to be

Climbing to the airy throne,
Where the Thunder sits alone.

Roland listened, confused, amazed,
While an unknown frenzy thrilled his heart;
And Agatha on the lady gazed
With steadfast eyes and lips apart;
And there sat the friar smoothing his beard,
As into the maiden's eyes he peered
With a sidelong sinister glance;
While she, as one in a charméd trance,
Bending forward, could only see
Roland leaning on the lady's knee,
With pale, bewildered countenance,
Gazing up in her face, which beamed
As if a torchlight on it gleamed;
And flushed as with an orient wine,
Where passion's swift and fitful flame
On the breath of music went and came
Like a gusty blaze on a heathen shrine.

"'Tis a sight to make a graybeard feel,"
Exclaimed the monk, "his old heart reel,
E'en though it beats in the breast of a friar!
Old age is a rust which may conceal;
But under it there is the tempered steel
Holding its latent spark of fire.

"See how he looks in the lady's face,
And how her dark eyes gloat on him!
In each other's soul they gaze, and trace
Thoughts which to us are vague and dim.

"Ah me! it recalls that hour divine,
In a palace garden at day's decline,
When a youth beneath a Sicilian vine
Sat with a lady, and she was crowned
With scarlet flowers and leaves embrowned,
Even as they had been seared to death
In the hot sirocco of passion's breath!

Oh, how she played! The hours were drowned
In goblets of music, and love, and wine!
But, well-a-day!—for that same sin
The youth became a Capuchin!"

VII.

Every word of the garrulous monk
Into the maiden's sad heart sunk,
With a dreary plunge and spasm
Sinking through the aching chasm,
As desperate shapes of agony
Leap from a burning ship at sea!
And as she gazed on the lovers there,
Every hope in her breast of despair—
Hopes which until now unknown
Had thronged her heart, with a sigh and a groan
Dropt away through the dusky waves
Low and lower to their briny graves,
With downward face and wide-spread hair!

Was it Love—or was it Hate—
The hate of bitter Jealousy—
Or conscious of being desolate—
Or was it the combinéd three
That thrilled the maiden suddenly,
Like variant winds that smite and wake
The waters of a summer lake?

"See!" said the lady with a glance of glee,
"How the dear child looks at us!
Why stares she so? Why breathes she thus?
As if her heart were parching to dust
In a roaring and raging furnace-gust!
Ah, Roland, it is plain to see
This is all for the love of thee!

"Oh, it is a pity and shame
To see a young heart thus consumed—
Even though it burns self-doomed
In an unrequited flame!"

Thus speaking, the lady with looks of pity,
Woke the prelude of a strange wild ditty;
Touching the lute with a gentler sweep,
She poured from her bosom, full and deep,
A burst of song that rose and fell
With a heavy and heated and stifling swell,
As fanned from a tropical garden in bloom
By the sultry wings of a far simoom!

"A princess dwelt beneath the sea,
    In a palace of coral and pearl;—
Her liquid chambers wide and free
Were lined with soft green tapestry,
Where a thousand suitors bent the knee;
    But her lip wore a scornful curl.

"There day by day she seemed to pine,
    In her palace of coral and pearl;—
Thronging the halls of the crystal brine,
In vain they came in a flattering line,

With the wealth of every Indian mine,
King, Prince and Duke and Earl.

"But her heart was wandering far away
From her palace of coral and pearl;—
Seeking the realm of the upper day,
Sighing as April sighs for May,
Through her emerald roof she saw the ray,
Like a flag at morn, unfurl.

"For she, like many a princess before,
In her palace of coral and pearl,
Had dreamed of one on a foreign shore,
The only one her soul could adore,
And thither her thoughts went more and more,
Till her weary brain 'gan whirl!

"'I pine,' she cried, 'alone, alone!'
In her palace of coral and pearl:—
'I pine and perish where hope is none!

Would I were sailing with the sun,
Would that the home of my love were won,
    Though he spurned me like a churl!

"'But like a dull sea-weed I cling
    To this palace of coral and pearl!—
Though round me the crystal alcoves ring
With praises my syren subjects sing,
Yet hopeless I pine as he were a king,
    And I a poor peasant-girl!'"

She ceased; but ere the sound had passed,
The skippers' voice, like a rattling blast
Blown through empty spar and shroud,
Announcing the tempest-bearing cloud,
Took up the strain, while he pressed the helm,
Still looking the lord of the watery realm;
And as he sung the instrument
Its wild accompanying cadence lent:—

"A monarch reigned beneath the sea
On the wreck of a myriad thrones,—
The collected ruins of Tyranny,
Shattered by the hand of Destiny,
And scattered abroad with maniac glee,
Like a gibbeted pirate's bones.

"Alone, supreme, he reigned apart,
On the throne of a myriad thrones,—
Where sitting close to the world's red heart,
Which pulsed swift heat through his ocean mart,
He could hear each heavy throe and start,
As she heaved her earthquake groans.

"He gazed through the shadowy deep which shields
His throne of a myriad thrones,—
And saw the many variant keels
Driving over the watery fields,
Some with thunderous and flashing wheels
Linking the remotest zones.

"Oft, like an eagle that swoops in air,
He saw from his throne of thrones,
The wingéd anchors with eager stare
Leap midway down to the ocean's lair—
While hanging plummets gazed in despair
At the unreached sands and stones!

"Along his realm lie mountainous bulks,
The tribute to his throne of thrones,—
The merchant's and the pirate's hulks,—
And where the ghost of the slaver skulks,
Counting his cargo,—then swears and sulks
Among the manacled bones!

"His navy numbers many a bark,
The pride of his throne of thrones:—
Golden by day and fiery by dark,
Each cleaves his pathway like a shark!
But his favourite barge is a dragon-ark,
The fairest ship he owns!

"The voice of that princess beneath the sea
Reached to his throne of thrones;—
Then he leaped in his barge right gallantly—
And cried, 'My child, come sail with me,
We will flash to sunward far and free,
Till love for thy grief atones!'"

The skipper ceased. 'Twas but a lull
In the gale of song! With bosom full
As some gigantic organ-bellows,
Worked by the hands of officious fellows,
While the priest at the altar white
Is slowly chanting a sacred rite,
The monk burst forth with a gusty roar,
That seemed to echo along the shore:—

"An abbot dwelt beneath the sea
In a cloister of shell and weed;—
Its walls of curious masonry
Were built by the ocean peasantry,

Those merman slaves, whose supple knee
Loves best a mysterious creed.

"And he was so virtuous, the story runs,
In his cloister of shell and weed—
That the pious mermen, fathers and sons,
Their daughters and sisters, the fairest ones,
Brought to his charge, till a thousand nuns
Chanted his mystical creed.

"And he had control of a thousand friars,
In his cloister of shell and weed;—
He taught them to chasten all worldly desires,
To smother with prayer all carnal fires;—
Not to be drunkards, and not to be liars,
Or gluttons of boundless greed!

"And warned them,—but this was a slander base,—
In his cloister of shell and weed,—
Not to be like that earthly race

Who had brought the system into disgrace,
Till the Devil himself grew red in the face
At sins he had never decreed!

"This abbot heard, through the sedgy grate
Of his cloister of shell and weed,
The woful princess bewailing her fate,
Then saw the approaching barge of state—
And closing his missal and locking his gate,
He leaped aboard with speed.

"A scion of Church and State was he,
In his cloister of shell and weed,—
And well he knew if a wedding should be,
That he as chief prelate under the sea,
Must be there to perform the solemn decree,
To sign and to seal the deed!"

VIII.

WHILE the songs were sung, each passing breath
Seemed breathed from the feverish breast of Death;
All the air which had heard the tune
Hung sultry and heavy and dead,
Pulsed through and through with flushes of red,
And hot as a broad, unshielded noon
In a fiery clime at the end of June.

In the purple sky, an hour too soon,
Like a wedding-bark await
At a Venetian palace-gate,
Floated the empty, crescent moon,
Moored at a crimson cloud,—a barge of state
In the sunset's broad lagune.

But to Agatha that cloud
Seemed like a world consuming with fire—
Whereon the avenging sun had breathed his ire!
And the moon was only a poor corpse in a shroud,
Which had been shot from a bark forlorn
Into the tranquil sea at morn,
That rose at eve a ghastly sight,
To blanch the mariner's cheek with fright!

Incongruous fancies, a maniac crowd,
Leaped through her brain, and shrieked aloud;
While, as to a blighting gust
Of red ashes and dust,
With a desperate wail her sad soul bowed.
And when with dry, hot eyes she saw—
Each throbbing like a burning heart—
The glowing lady lean and draw
Roland close to her heaving side,
And smoothing his floating locks apart,
With looks of mingled passion and pride,

Press on his brow a heated kiss,—
Her heart, as one in a nightmare dream,
Striving with fruitless effort to scream,
Seemed plunging down a black abyss.

But when the lady, with sidelong eyes
Half-veiled in mocking hate's eclipse,—
A look which pitied, yet seemed to despise—
Glanced at the maiden's face of despair,
And bending down and down with triumphant air,
Set the hot seal of her love on his lips—
There was more than a frenzied soul could bear!
A sudden shriek—wild, sharp, and shrill!
A plunge!—a gurgle!—a widening thrill
Rippling the water! And all was still!

"Oh, see!" cried the lady,—"O Roland, behold!
She has leapt in the sea!
She is drowned in the sea!
And it is all for the love of thee!

Her heart was so warm, and your blood was so cold!"
"By Heaven!" he cried, "it shall not be!"
Then another plunge and another thrill
Rippled the wave; and a voice as shrill
As ever a fiend could shout in glee,
Cried, "Adieu! adieu!
Till we meet anew
In our palace of splendour far under the sea!"

And all the air, the moment after,
Was filled with wild demoniac laughter—
And like swift hounds in pursuit of a wolf,
Sudden flaws from the leash of the gale
Leapt upon the straining sail,
And chased it over the flashing gulf.
Away and away, with a murderous flight,
Sped the bark,—away and away!
Doubling the headland into the bay,
Like a red-handed homicide flying from sight!

IX.

The toil, the danger and despair
Struggling with hope in that brief moment there,
May not be chronicled or said;
Or how it seemed from ocean's shadowy bed
That demon shapes leapt up, with murderous hands,
Striving to pluck the desperate swimmer down,
That with his burden he might sink and drown,
And lie supine upon the charnel sands.

But still he laboured; — and a form divine,
Such as an angel clothed in sunshine hath,
Glimmered before him, walking on the brine —
Slow leading shoreward in a golden path.
And well he knew 'twas that sweet pitying sprite
Which he had driven into the howling night!

But now her pale lips seemed to move
Forgivingly with smiles of love,—
Until his heart with hope beat high and warm,
And a new impulse nerved his struggling arm.

Anon his feet were on the slanting sands,
Where slow he toiled with the increasing weight,
Which, like a sea-weed stranded, desolate,
Hung o'er his arm with dripping hair and hands.
And now wild groups came down the sloping lands,
Looming gigantic 'gainst the level sun,
And their long shadows to the beach did run
Precipitate with uncontrollèd wo—
Outstripping those who followed! Till anon
Around the melancholy show
The people gathered, and with faces wan
Told their great grief as only mourners can
Who loved the thing they mourn from the hour its
life began!

Foremost her sire, a wild disconsolate man,
Mingled with the wet grief of the sea
The tears of his tempest agony,
Which like baptismal waters ran
Over her breathless breast, as from the hand
Of the pale priestess Sorrow flung,
Naming her one of that most enviable band
Whom loving Death has ta'en into his land
While beautiful and young—
Into the land of May, forever green,
To be crowned with virgin flowers immortally a queen.

With shreds of white hair sorrowing in the breeze,
The village priest leant o'er her with a prayer;
And then he said, "Let loving arms of care
Take up this mournful victim of the seas,
And bear her to the church, and on a bier
Lay her before the sacred altar-shrine,
Where the mild Saviour, with His eyes divine,
Looks peace to grief, and hope to those who fear;

And as he lifted Jairus' child from death,
He may renew even here the life-reviving breath."
And as he bade they bore her; while behind
Pale Roland followed with bewildered mind.

X.

When they had gained the little chapel door,
And were about to cross the sacred sill,
Their drownéd burden, breathless as before,
The anxious crowd beheld, with sudden thrill,
The serpent ring her dripping right-hand bore
Leap from her finger and as lightning pass,
Flashing between their feet,
Searing the ground with heat,
A crooked flame that vanished in the grass.

Then straightway to the maiden's cheek
Flushed up a little dawn of life;

And her waking pulses, weary and weak,
In their recovery seemed to speak
Of the long and maddening strife,
Of the maniac dreams which had filled her brain,
While her heart lay stunned in its night of pain.

And when at the altar-shrine
They laid her like a corpse supine,
Scarce noting the life-announcing sign,
Then Roland fell on his knees, and pressed
Her cold white hands to his aching breast:
And instantly the long frozen pain
Which had oppressed and benumbed his brain,
Seemed to melt in a repentant glow,
And in floods of tears to his eyelids flow,
Till his sad heart felt like an arid plain
That is drenched with a generous summer rain.

Was it the sunset's parting beam
Piercing the little window red?

Or was it the lightning's vivid gleam
Through the startled twilight shed?
They only knew a crimson flush,
Making the sacred shadows blush,
Shot up the aisle, as if the fiery rays
Of a meteor-ball had set the air ablaze:
And then a baleful voice
Drew their eyes to the door away;
And all could plainly hear it say,
"Come, Roland, come! Thou hast no choice:
Thou shalt not, darest not stay:
The prayer which thou must learn to pray
At another altar must be made,
And thy vows to another God be paid!"

And gazing through the door, they saw
The lady and monk beyond the sill;
And every breast was filled with awe,
And every pulse ran chill.

They stood like travellers in the night,
Surrounded by a blazing light,
Who see the eyes of the wolf and pard,
Fixed with wild and eager desire,
Insane with hunger, and only debarred
By a living threshold of circling fire.

Then Roland cried, "Avaunt! avaunt!
Here at this holy altar I swear,
By my future hopes and my past despair,
To fly from the fiends and that lonely haunt,
With pain, and wo, and demons rife!
And if once this sweet maid come to life,
To claim her my bride! And in token of this,
I set on her lips this sealing kiss!"

He spake and bowed—lips touched to lips;
And as a taper, when the gusty dark
Has blown its splendour into eclipse,
While its wick still holds the crimson spark,

Which, touching another taper's rays,
Instantly stands in the air ablaze,—
So life, in a swift contagious flame,
Suddenly illumined the maiden's frame!

A moment surveying the sacred place,
Her blue eyes turned, then with modest grace
Gazing up into Roland's face,
Her sweet tongue said, in its first release,
With words which seemed breathed from the lips
of peace—
"The spell is past! Oh, hour divine!
Thou, thou art mine! and I am thine!"

And the listening shadows cool and gray,
In the gallery, like a responding choir,
Where the organ glowed like an altar-fire,
Seemed to the echoing vault to say,
Softly as at a nuptial shrine—
"Thou art mine! and I am thine!"

And still through the breathless moments after,
Like doves beneath the sheltering rafter,
Along the roof in faint decline,
The echoes whispered with voices fine—
"Mine and thine! mine and thine!"

And now, like a golden trumpet, blown
To make a glorious victory known,
The organ with its roll divine,
Poured abroad from its thrilling tongue
Words the sweetest ever sung—
"Mine and thine! mine and thine!"

And up in the tower the iron bell
Suddenly felt the joyous spell,
And flung its accents clear and gay,
As if it were rung on a wedding-day;
And like a singer swaying his head
To mark the time
Of some happy rhyme,

Breathing his heart in every line,
Thus swayed the bell, and swaying said—
"Mine and thine! mine and thine!"

XI.

THE lady standing beyond the door,
Like one whose despair can bear no more,
Shrieked a fiendish shriek of wrath;
And, with a hollow sepulchral sound,
Her body fell upon the ground
And lay a corpse along the path!

And then a shadow, like a cloud
On a hissing whirlwind fierce and loud,
Swept seaward, pierced with curses and shrieks,
Which like the lightning's fiery streaks
Flashed madly through the twilight shades,
Cleaving the air with sulphurous blades!

Then the people ran to the headland height
With the fascination of wonder and fright,—
And saw the little dragon bark,
Speeding out to the eastern dark —
Away and away, as swift and bright
As a red flamingo's sudden flight.

And climbing the black rocks high and higher
They gazed and gazed with aching sight,—
Till into the distant realm of night
They saw it pass — a ship on fire!

Then Roland, who gazed on the body which lay
In the path, a loathsome shape of clay,
Defiled by a fiend and cast away,
Called to the sturdy sacristan,
Who came, a shuddering, awe-struck man,
And bade him with his graveyard crew
Bear and bury the thing from view.

But when they strove, with fear and disgust,
To raise that form which once had been
The temple of Beauty and then of Sin,
It fell from their hands a mass of dust,—
Like a cavern of sand, so fragile and thin,
That a single touch will shatter it in;—
Or like a long-consumèd brand,
Whose form in the ashes seems to stand,
From whence the hungry flame has fled
And left it a thing devoured and dead,
Which the lightest touch of the lifting hand
Shivers to nothing, a shapeless mass;—
Thus the body fell, and lay on the grass
A crumbled pile at their startled feet,
As if it had been consumed by the heat
Of that most subtle and fiery fiend
Which so long it had fearfully harboured and screened!

Days dawned and set, and year by year
The bride became more fair and dear;
And Roland saw with secret delight,
As her face grew more refined and bright,
How through every feature it seemed
That the light of his long-lost Ida beamed!
And by degrees her softening voice
Like Ida's made his heart rejoice;
Until, when the first few years had flown,
He forgot that his early love had died,
And walking at his lady's side,
He called her "Ida," and she replied
To the name as it had been her own.

Never more to that lonely height,
Where only the wild birds of the sea
Peopled the gusty balcony,
He turned his feet; but lived and moved
Among his fellows—revered, beloved;

And the world was no more a world of blight,
But a realm of sunshine, warm and bright.
With his brooding grief no longer blind,
This simple truth his soul discerned,—
And well it were for all mankind
Had they the selfsame lesson learned,—
That it is not in the world abroad,
In the sight of men and the light of God,
That fierce temptations chiefly dwell;
But in the misanthropic cell,
Where the selfish passions are all enshrined
And worshipped by one darksome mind.

THE END.

STEREOTYPED BY L. JOHNSON & CO.
PHILADELPHIA

READ'S ILLUSTRATED POEMS.

Poems, by T. BUCHANAN READ. A new and enlarged edition. Beautifully illustrated with designs by eminent artists, and finely engraved on steel. Cloth, extra, gilt edge - - - - - - - $3.50

Turkey morocco - - - - - - - 6.00

Cloth, without illustrations - - - 1.00

"*We do not hesitate to declare our opinion that* Mr. READ *is the most promising of the living transatlantic poets.* We know of no other American (with the doubtful exception of Edgar Poe) having so much real feeling as is shown in some of his verses. It presents a refreshing contrast with the cold and clever manufactures which most of his contemporaries would impose upon us as expressions of feeling. Mr. READ has a very high sense of natural beauty: this kind of description is his *forte*. We offer no apology for quoting the whole of the exquisite poem called 'The Closing Scene.' *This is unquestionably the best American poem we have met with; indeed it is, with one or two exceptions, the only American poem we have read, or could have read over and over again.* It is an addition to the permanent stock of poetry in the English language. The first thirteen stanzas, taken by themselves, constitute a truly inspired little poem. Tennyson himself, the great modern master of that kind of description which employs the object of outward nature as a language for human feeling, has scarcely surpassed, in its way, this poem, *which in our opinion merits the fame that Gray's celebrated 'Elegy' has obtained, without deserving it nearly so well.* The feeling of the three opening stanzas—the only unexceptionable passage of more than two or three lines in Gray's poem—is here sustained to a far greater length, and with much simpler language and imagery. Mr. READ'S volume affords other equally remarkable instances of perception and polish."—*North British Review.*

"It is pleasant to turn to a volume of poetry like Mr. READ'S, and not the less so, as enabling us to pay a most willing tribute to American genius. When an American poet is not only known but reprinted here, it is clear that his genius is of a more universal and general character, touching the heart as such, not as an American or English heart. Pure, tender, sympathizing, and hopeful, with an eye observant of nature and an ear well trained to give melodious expression to every turn of thought—simple and unpretending in the choice of subjects, but touching each with fresh, genuine feeling—there are not many modern writers of verse who have supplied us with such a pleasant book of desultory reading. * * * * One poem, called 'The Closing Scene,' in which the thoughts, measure, and cadence are in happy harmony, we are obliged unwillingly to curtail. A description of late and dreary Autumn, given with American accuracy of scene-painting, ushers in a picture of failing and sorrowful humanity."—*Christian Remembrancer, (a London Quarterly Review.)*

"A poet, whose fame, both at home and abroad, heightens with each successive production, and widens as the knowledge of his work extends."—*Willis & Morris's Home Journal.*

"The volume we have now the pleasure of introducing to our readers abounds with delicately-pictured images, a rich, luxuriant fancy, and high-toned sentiments, marked by a touching and polished simplicity. * * * All is mirrored in the poet's soul like the beautifully brilliant foliage which his genius pictures on the bosom of the quiet stream or sequestered lake."—*American Courier*

THE NEW PASTORAL.

A Poem. By THOS. BUCHANAN READ. 1 vol. 12mo, cloth - - - - - - - - - - $1.00

"We must give Mr. READ the credit for writing the only good pastoral poem of the present day."—*Evening Bulletin.*

"Poetically imagined and beautifully expressed."—*Baltimore American.*

"It will be welcomed as the *first* truly American poem. We predict for it an immense circulation. It must become one of the indispensables for the centre-table in America, both in the palace and the cottage."—*Farm Journal.*

"The New Pastoral supplies the vacant place in the literature of America, which Thomson and Cowper have filled in that of England; and we feel proud of our young countryman when we say, equally well. His poem is purely national—American in its scope, in its spirit, in its ideas, and in the exquisite pictures of rural life and manners which constitute its chief charm."—*Reading Democrat.*

"Mr. READ has given us a pastoral poem of great smoothness of versification, naturalness of thought and expression, and abounding in passages of great beauty; while over the whole is breathed a spirit of domestic and rustic quietude such as commends it to the gentler sympathies of the soul. It deserves to take its place among the best of our fireside poetry."—*N. Y. Observer.*

"American literature gets, in *The New Pastoral*, a valuable acquisition."—*Boston Transcript.*

"The author has, by this work, achieved for himself a high position among American poets. * * * It will continue a 'standard' in the literature of his country. * * * A chastened imagination has decked homely scenes with all the charms which it is the high power of poesy only to do, and painted American rural changes with a lifelike fidelity which stamps them forever upon the page."—*Morning News.*

"We have the 'New Pastoral,' from the pen of THOMAS BUCHANAN READ, a poet whose name and fame bid fair to become household words in America. In simple and flutelike prolongations of melody it breathes the soul of a new people, stirred by new experiences, dwelling in a fresh, young world."—*Commercial Register.*

"The *North British Review* pronounced one of Mr. READ'S former productions the best poem that had appeared from an American author. We think the poet's well-merited reputation will not suffer from the present work. It is rich in the elements of a permanent popularity. The just appreciation of nature; the beauty of description; the truthful pictures of simple, rural life; the delicacy of sentiment; the overflowing of a gentle, loving heart, and the sweetly flowing numbers, cannot fail to win admirers, and gain new laurels for the bard. The fact that it is also, in all respects, a home production, thoroughly American in all its incidents and scenery, gives it additional charms."—*Presbyterian.*

"It is written with sincerity and feeling: there are descriptions which have great truth of detail. and the poem has the great merit of a subdued and natural tone."—*Putnam's Monthly.*

"The lovers of sound moral sentiment most sweetly expressed, and of the bright portraiture of nature in her peaceful scenes and moods, will find in this volume a great deal to elevate, to interest, and to refine."—*Natchez Courier.*

A Survey of the Literature of the United States.

BY RUFUS WILMOT GRISWOLD.

I. THE POETS AND POETRY OF AMERICA.
II. THE FEMALE POETS OF AMERICA.
III. THE PROSE WRITERS OF AMERICA.

THE POETS AND POETRY OF AMERICA,

By RUFUS W. GRISWOLD. Containing Biographical and Critical Memoirs, and the best Poems of all the best Poets. Sixteenth edition. With Portraits on Steel of Dana, Bryant, Percival, Longfellow, Gallagher, Poe, Cooke, Lowell, Taylor. Carefully revised, re-arranged, much enlarged, and brought down to the year 1855. 1 vol. royal 8vo, cloth, gilt - $3.00

"It is performing a valuable service when a man of taste and information makes a suitable, well-assorted selection, and guides the friend of poetry in his rambles through those groves from which he might otherwise be deterred by their immensity. Such service has been rendered by Mr. GRISWOLD in his 'Poets and Poetry of America.'"—*From Baron* FREDERICK VON RAUMER, *of Prussia.*

"We doubt whether there is another man in America who could have been found to devote so much industry, not to say drudgery, as was called for in such an undertaking. Sure we are that no such man could have been found who would have done it so well."—*From the New York Courier and Enquirer.*

"The editor has executed his task with industry, skill, and taste. No man in this country is probably so familiar with this branch of American literature, not only in regard to its most ancient, but most obscure authors."—*From the New York Evening Post.*

"No collection of American poetry at all comparable to it in extent, completeness, or general merit, has ever been issued."—*From the Albany Evening Journal.*

"Mr. GRISWOLD has succeeded as well in his book as the nature of the case admitted. His patient research and general correctness of taste are worthy of praise; his difficulties and temptations would have extenuated far graver errors than he has committed, and his volume well deserves the approbation it has received."—*From the North American Review, (by* E. P. WHIPPLE.)

"We must not forget to thank Mr. GRISWOLD for his good taste and good feeling. It would be difficult to overpraise either."—*From the London Examiner.*

"We think in this beautiful volume the reader will find nearly all that is worth reading in American poetry."—*From the Boston Morning Post.*

"Mr. GRISWOLD'S work is honourable to the character and genius of the American people."—*From* THOS. CAMPBELL, *author of "The Pleasures of Hope."*

"The critical and biographical notes are brief, but discriminative and elegant."—*From Bishop* POTTER'S *"Hand-Book for Readers."*

THE FEMALE POETS OF AMERICA,

By RUFUS W. GRISWOLD. Containing extended Critical and Biographical Notices, with Poems, Chronologically Arranged. Fifth edition: continued to 1856. With Portraits on Steel of Maria Brooks, Frances S. Osgood, Alice Carey, Julia Ward Howe, &c. 1 vol. royal 8vo, cloth, gilt - - - - - - $3.00

"Very rare, and very opposite, and very high abilities are required for that circumnavigation of the whole continent of literature—that exploration of every bay, and river, and inland lake, with all their islands—that picturesque representation of every peculiarity of the subjects of research, sketchy yet faithful, spirited yet minute—and, above all, that grouping of the whole in one historical picture of national genius, which are demanded by the enterprise which Dr. GRISWOLD has essayed, and which he has so successfully accomplished by a combination of knowledge and skill as uncommon as it is delightful. His biographical narratives display a great deal of spirit and tact. His criticisms exhibit a thorough familiarity with the writings which he reviews, and are animated with sensibilities and perceptions kindred in their delicacy and ardour with that inspiration from which the verses themselves have flowed. They are searching, truthful, comprehensive, and candid in their character, and always graceful and elegant in style."—*From the New York Tribune.*

"Of all Mr. GRISWOLD'S various works, the present evinces the greatest triumph over difficulties, and best demonstrates the minuteness and the extent of his knowledge of American literature. Very few of the women included in this collection have ever published editions of their writings, and a considerable portion of the verse was published anonymously. The labour, therefore, of collecting the materials of both the biographies and the illustrative extracts, must have been of that arduous and vexatious kind which only enthusiasm for the subject could have sustained. The volume is an important original contribution to the literary history of the country; and nobody, whose mind is not incurably vitiated by prejudice, can make dissimilarity of opinion with regard to some of the judgments expressed in the book, a ground for denying its general ability, honesty, and value. Most of the materials are strictly new, and this fact of itself is sufficient to stamp the work with that character which distinguishes books of original research from mere compilations."—*From Graham's American Monthly Magazine.*

"Dr. GRISWOLD has performed the duties of his undertaking with a diligence, a taste, and a discrimination, which we doubt whether any other man in this country could have equalled. The selections are copious and judicious, and the criticisms upon them are delicate and just. A great deal of trouble has obviously been taken to obtain materials for the work, and to bring together accurate information in regard to the authors. A very large portion of the poems have been given to the editor expressly for this collection. The work has, therefore, to a great extent, the value of an original production by the combined efforts of our female poets."—*From* MORRIS *and* WILLIS'S *Home Journal.*

"It is an erudite and elaborate review of the contributions of American women to that department of literature in which women may be expected to win the greatest triumphs. It is full of curious and entertaining information and genial and elegant criticism; and among its contents are nearly one hundred new poems, by our most distinguished female writers."—*From the N. American.*

The Prose Writers of America,

With an Introductory Survey of the Intellectual History, Condition, and Prospects of the Country. By RUFUS W. GRISWOLD. Illustrated with Portraits of Edwards, Irving, Audubon, Story, Wilde, Prescott, Kennedy, Emerson, and Hoffman. 1 vol. royal 8vo, cloth, gilt - - - - - - - - - - $3.00

"It will be an important and interesting contribution to our national literature. The range of authors is very wide, the biographical notices full and interesting. I am surprised that the author has been able to collect so many particulars in this way. The selections appear to me to have been made with discrimination, and the criticism shows a sound taste and a correct appreciation of the qualities of the writers, as well as I can judge."—*From* WM. H. PRESCOTT, *author of "Ferdinand and Isabella."*

"Dr. RUFUS W. GRISWOLD is the most learned bibliographer in the country. His book is a welcome one to us, and we presume will be so to the public, completing, as it does, the view of American literature of which his other work—The Poets of America—formed the first part. We confess that we do not agree with Dr. GRISWOLD'S estimate of some of the authors whose names appear in this work. We have, however, been long enough conversant with the literary world, to tolerate great latitude of opinion in regard to the merits of authors, and have ceased long ago to quarrel with those who do not happen to think of our favourite writers as we do, or who praise, as we imagine, without good cause. We are glad to possess, in this form, portions of many authors whose entire works we should never own, and, if we did, should probably never find time to read. We confess our obligations to the author also for the personal information concerning them which he has collected in the memoirs prefixed to their writings. These are written in a manner creditable to the research, ability, and kindness of the author."—*From the New York Evening Post, (by* Mr. BRYANT.)

"The design has been executed with candour, discrimination, and unquestionable ability. It has raised our opinion of Mr. GRISWOLD'S literary powers far beyond any estimate which we had formed from his previous efforts. There is a range of sympathy, a variety of knowledge, and a breadth and comprehensiveness of taste, which few men in the country could have exhibited. The independence of thought and fearlessness of criticism which are displayed are eminently worthy of commendation, on a subject and in a country where there is so great a lack of both. The introductory sketch is written with an ardent *amor patriæ*, and sets the literary pretensions of the country upon as high a ground as they can be placed by any man; and, whether it be that we partake of Mr. GRISWOLD'S national partiality, or have been stirred by his glowing interest, it has appeared to us, as we read, that his claims for American genius and art were not beyond the measure of truth and justice. His notices of several of the authors are as able specimens of particular criticism as we are acquainted with."—*From* MORRIS *and* WILLIS'S *Home Journal.*

"The book now before us is more than respectable: it is executed ably, and in many parts brilliantly. In some respects it is an extraordinary work, such as few men in America, perhaps, except the author, could have produced, and he only after years of sedulous investigation and under many advantages of circumstance or accident. The distribution of the various writers into their classes, and the selection of representatives of each class, or type, exhibit much skill."—*From the Knickerbocker, (by the late* HORACE BINNEY WALLACE.)

TAM'S FORTNIGHT RAMBLE.

Tam's Fortr ˙ ;ht Ramble, and other Poems. By THOMAS MACKELLAR. 216 pages, 12mo - - - - $0.75

"He is a man of genius, with a heart as tender as a woman's, who would have been effeminate from over-delicacy of construction, but for the masculine necessity of getting a livelihood. I like him."—N. P. WILLIS.

"Many of his sonnets bear upon them the richness of genius, and awaken those feelings which nothing but true poetry can arouse."—Hon. J. R. CHANDLER.

"We hesitate not to pronounce him a genuine poet."—Rev. J. W. ALEXANDER, D.D.

"Tam is no new acquaintance, either to us or to our readers; but one of those "old, familiar" friends who are cherished in our heart's core. The beauty of his verse, not less than of his sentiments, has endeared him to thousands on thousands of the readers of the *Gazette;* and not unfrequently his cheerful strains, his poetry "tipped with heavenliness," has made festival in many a sorrowing heart. Tam, or Mr. MACKELLAR, to speak of him by his real name, is no pretty trifler in verse, but an earnest man, writing on earnest subjects, and striving to do good as well as to amuse. Such should ever be the high aim of poetry." —J. C. NEAL, *editor of Neal's Gazette.*

"He touches every subject with ease and grace, and breathes life into that which was before inanimate."—*Del. Co. Repub.*

"Written by our printer-poet, as the title indicates, in a season of relief from the persecution of publishers, printers, and proofs. The poetry is remarkable for its beautiful simplicity, high-toned morality, and earnest piety."—Rev. Dr. SUMMERS.

"Mr. MACKELLAR has in him the poetry of pleasantry and pathos. Some passages are touching, others amusing, and all evincing sound sense and discrimination. A religious vein runs through all, and the minor poems are the breathings of a heart which seems to have the highest enjoyments amidst the domestic circle."—*Presbyterian, (Phila.)*

"This is a volume of poetry, in the best sense of the word; true poetry, responsive to nature and life, and to the heart of man. There is a charm—it is the power of inspiration—the charm of truth and nature, and of poetic feeling, blended with sacred charity—on almost every page, which invites and holds the willing eye and ear of the reader."—*Christian Observer.*

"He is a poet of nature and of the home affections, and he appeals to the heart with a gentle and persuasive force that only those who feel what they write can exercise. It is refreshing to turn from the stilted rhymes and forced ideas of most of the writers of the present day, to the sweet and pleasant thoughts that come upward from his heart to stir our sympathies and exact our admiration."—*Evening News.*

"The head and the heart of this author, although he is too modest to make high claims for either, in truth require no gratuitous commendation. His muse has indeed the truth, and depth, and insight of poetry, lacking only the passionateness, fire, and rapture with which its sometimes grandeur, oftener giddiness. intoxicates the fancy. It is a gentle, loving, hopeful, healthy heartiness that is the charm of his poems. The rhythm is smooth, the versification accurate, and the sentiment always beautiful. Extracts made anywhere at random from this book would show how just the character we ascribe to the writer, and how tame the praise we have given to his poetry."—Dr. ELDER.

Reed's Lectures on English Literature.

Lectures on English Literature, delivered in the Chapel Hall of the University of Pennsylvania by Professor Henry Reed. With a Portrait. Edited by his brother, William B. Reed. 1 vol. 12mo, cloth - $1.25

[*Extracts of a letter from Professor* C. C. Felton, *of Harvard.*]

Cambridge, *May* 21, 1855.

Gentlemen:

I have read, with much pleasure and instruction, the Lectures of the late Professor Reed, on English Literature, published by you.

Among the greatest improvements made in our higher schools within a few years, there is none, in my opinion, more important than the increased attention paid to the study of English Literature, as an essential element of education. * * * * As a guide and companion in this department of education, the volume of Professor Reed's Lectures appears to me truly admirable. The subject is treated in a comprehensive and able manner. The style of the Lectures is pure and graceful: the criticism judicious: the general principles clearly stated, and illustrated with careful thought and comprehensive study: the moral and religious tone is every thing that could be desired for a work to be put into the hands of the young; and I know of no book, in that department of elegant letters, better suited to cultivate and purify the taste, and to excite the enthusiasm of pupils.

I am, gentlemen, very respectfully, yours, C. C. FELTON.

Messrs. Parry & McMillan.

"The book is in every way a most creditable contribution to the Library of Critical Literature."—*London Leader.*

"These Lectures bear the marks of ripe scholarship and an accomplished mind."—*Presbyterian.*

"The Lectures are of the highest order, both in scholarship, sound sense, and gracefulness of style, and show a thorough mastery of his subject that only a familiar acquaintance with the original sources could have given. There is also a moral purity and a Christian spirit running through them that is peculiarly pleasing."—*Watchman and Observer.*

"* * * * If any thing could bring consolation to the friends of Professor Reed for his untimely loss, it is that he left his MSS. in such a complete and scholar-like preparation that the public will receive them as a national benefit. * * * * The third lecture of the volume, on the English language, is in itself a monument of the varied and extensive learning and acquirements of the lamented author, which would hand down his name to posterity as one of the gifted of the nineteenth century."—*National Intelligencer.*

"A posthumous work, and a noble monument to the memory of the distinguished Professor, whose loss in the Arctic created such an intense sorrow in the city of his birth, education, and active life, and such an overwhelming sense of calamity wherever his just fame had spread."—*Home Journal.*

"These lectures, or rather essays, are of surpassing beauty and excellence. We know not where to look for a volume so admirably adapted to the wants of a large class of young readers, who desire to direct their reading intelligently and profitably."—*Boston Traveller.*

Lectures on English History,

As illustrated by Shakspeare's Chronicle Plays, and on Tragic Poetry. By Henry Reed. Edited by his brother, William B. Reed. 1 vol. 12mo - $1.25

"Beginning with the dim legendary period on which Lear and Cymbeline shed a few rays of light, Mr. Reed, in these exquisite essays—for such, rather than lectures, they are—traces the varied course of English history down to the verge of the Poet's own day—the reign of Henry the Eighth and the birth of Elizabeth; and it is wonderful to be made to understand, by the continuity of such a mode of illustration, how complete the course is. Marlborough's confession of ignorance was not so great as one is apt to think, when he said that all he knew of English history he learned from Shakspeare's plays; and Mr. Reed shows us now how complete, and thorough, and accurate, the Poet's knowledge was. There is throughout a happy blending of criticism and history, and withal, in perhaps a greater degree than in Mr. Reed's former volume, that transparency of style which reveals in every page the pure and gentle character, the strong intelligence and high morality, of the author. No one that begins this little book will lay it down till it is finished. It is, too, suited to all tastes and all ages."—*North American.*

"We welcome another valuable contribution to English *belles-lettres*, from the papers of the late Professor Henry Reed. With happy originality, the historical plays of Shakspeare are made the basis of lectures upon English history—not the less instructive because adorned with all the graces of poetry. The theme is thus relieved from any scholastic dulness, and made attractive to those who read for amusement, as well as to severe students. * * * * The present volume is invested with much of the interest of a personal memoir, by the judicious introduction of extracts from the private correspondence of the lamented author."—*City Item.*

"In this work, the lovers of English literature and English history again have the privilege of reading the emanations of one of the most cultivated minds of which our country can boast. Professor Reed's style is beautifully chaste and powerfully correct—possessing none of those redundances which are like a withered branch, but close yet free, elegant, but not youthfully florid. * * * * It is no ordinary work, but one that from its importance marks an era in literature."—*Pennsylvanian.*

"Professor Reed has gained a transatlantic reputation of which any one might be proud; and it is enough for the work before us to say that it will add in a high degree to that reputation. * * * * These Lectures require no praise. No one can read them without adding materially to his stock of information, or without being impressed by the judicious relation of facts, the taste in illustration, or the purity of language everywhere displayed."—*Bulletin.*

"These Lectures show a knowledge not only of the text of England's greatest bard, but a deep and critical examination of their suggestions, and we believe will be found to be of inestimable value, as commentaries upon the genius of him who has long puzzled the acumen of scholars, and given food for thought to the great minds of every age. That they are valuable additions to the historical literature of our country, no one who knows Professor Reed's ability can for a moment doubt. * * * * For the collection of his works we are indebted to the affectionate regard of his brother, William B. Reed, Esq.; and we cannot take leave of the volume without expressing our satisfaction with the manner in which that gentleman has executed the task."—*Argus.*

www.ingramcontent.com/pod-product-compliance
Lightning Source LLC
LaVergne TN
LVHW021404110826
845150LV00007B/1775

9781425512040